BABY ANIMALS

BABY
GIRAFFES

by K.C. Kelley

AMICUS

neck

hooves

Look for these
words and pictures
as you read.

spots

tongue

Who is getting a kiss?
It's a baby giraffe!

A baby giraffe is called a calf.
At birth, they are
6 feet (1.8 m) tall!

See the baby's spots?
Giraffes have many spots.
No two spots are alike.

spots

tongue

See its tongue?
Baby giraffes have long tongues.
They use them to grab plants.

Look at its hooves.

Baby giraffes have four legs.

Their feet are called hooves.

hooves

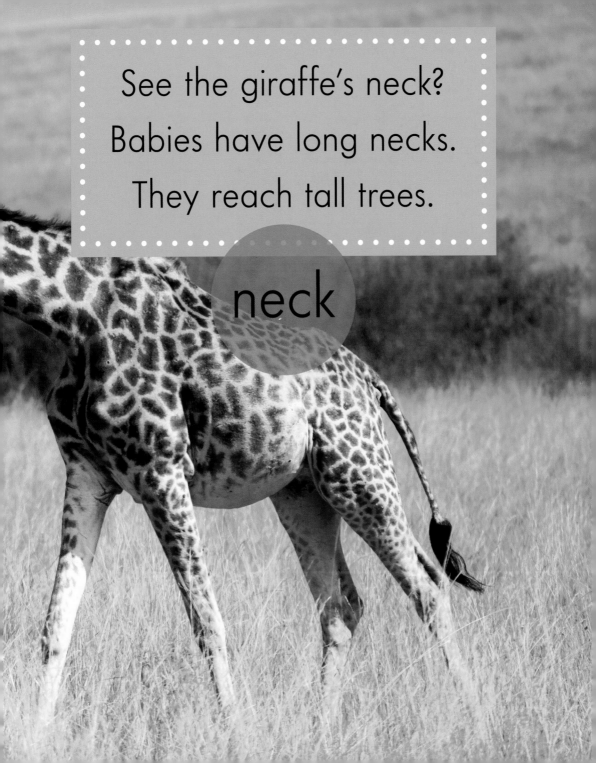

See the giraffe's neck?
Babies have long necks.
They reach tall trees.

neck

Baby giraffes live in Africa.
They stay safe in groups.
Time for a drink!

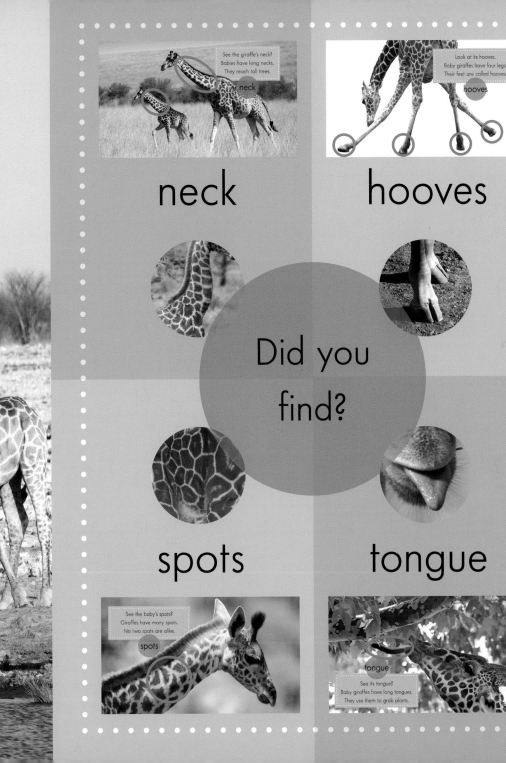

neck

hooves

Did you find?

spots

tongue

Amicus Readers and Amicus Ink are imprints of Amicus
P.O. Box 1329, Mankato, MN 56002
www.amicuspublishing.us

Library of Congress Cataloging-in-Publication Data
Names: Kelley, K. C., author.
Title: Baby giraffes / by K.C. Kelley.
Description: Mankato, MN : Amicus, [2018] | Series: Spot baby
animals
Identifiers: LCCN 2017022571 (print) | LCCN 2017031873
(ebook) | ISBN
  9781681513331 (pdf) | ISBN 9781681513195 (library binding
: alk. paper) |
  ISBN 9781681522531 (pbk. : alk. paper)
Subjects: LCSH: Giraffe--Infancy--Juvenile literature.
Classification: LCC QL737.U56 (ebook) | LCC QL737.U56 K454
2018 (print) | DDC
  599.63813/92--dc23
LC record available at https://lccn.loc.gov/2017022571

Printed in China

HC 10 9 8 7 6 5 4 3 2 1
PB 10 9 8 7 6 5 4 3 2 1

Megan Peterson, editor
Deb Miner, series designer
Patty Kelley, book designer
Producer/Photo Research:
Shoreline Publishing Group LLC

Photos:
Cover: Andrey Gudkov/
Dreamstime.com.
Inside: Dreamstime.com:
Dragoneye 1, David Bate
2tl, Amilevin 2tr, Colette6,
Henkbentlage 2br, Andrey
Gudkov 3, Simon Fletcher
4, Alexander Shalamov 6,
Aragami12345 8, Richard Koele
10, Serrnovik 12, Smellme 14.

BABY
GIRAFFES